iMath
Readers

Hidden Ducks:
Describing and Interpreting Data

by Renata Brunner-Jass

Content Consultant
David T. Hughes
Mathematics Curriculum Specialist

NORWOOD HOUSE PRESS
Chicago, IL

Norwood House Press
PO Box 316598
Chicago, IL 60631

For information regarding Norwood House Press, please visit our website at
www.norwoodhousepress.com or call 866-565-2900.

Special thanks to: Heidi Doyle
Production Management: Six Red Marbles
Editors: Linda Bullock and Kendra Muntz
Printed in Heshan City, Guangdong, China. 208N—012013

Paperback ISBN: 978-1-60357-511-9

The Library of Congress has cataloged the original hardcover edition with the following call number: 2012034492

CONTENTS

Note to Caregivers:

Throughout this book, many questions are posed to the reader. Some are open-ended and ask what the reader thinks. Discuss these questions with your child and guide him or her in thinking through the possible answers and outcomes. There are also questions posed which have a specific answer. Encourage your child to read through the text to determine the correct answer. Most importantly, encourage answers grounded in reality while also allowing imaginations to soar. Information to help support you as you share the book with your child is provided in the back in the **Additional Notes** section.

Bold words are defined in the glossary in the back of the book.

Math Camp!

Each summer, many students attend a day camp program at a nearby state park. The program is called Math Camp. The students have fun using math to learn about the park and nature. They also get to do other outdoor activities.

The park is an amazing place! It's huge. It includes a lake, so there are lots of water activities. There are many miles of hiking trails that wind through forests and meadows. People can visit for a day, having picnics and taking day hikes. They can also camp in the park or take longer **backpacking** trips.

In Math Camp, we work with people who work at the park, called **rangers**. Together, we observe people and wildlife. We learn how people like to use the park. We work in teams to gather **data**, or information. We practice describing the data and figuring out what they mean.

Describing Data

Data are information, usually in the form of numbers. A **data point** is one piece of information in a set of data. Often, a single number can be used to describe a set of data. For example, a group of Math Camp students counted the number of visitors to the gift shop one week.

	Sun.	Mon.	Tue.	Wed.	Thu.	Fri.	Sat.
Number of Visitors	80	68	101	92	76	72	232

Idea 1: Find the Range. The **range** is the difference between the least and greatest values in a set of data. The greatest value in the chart above is 232. The least value is 72. The range of these data is 160.

Idea 2: Find the Median. The **median** is the number that falls in the exact middle of a set of data. In the case of an even number of data, the median is the **average** of the two middle values. To find the median of a set of data, order the data from least to greatest value:

$$68 \quad 72 \quad 76 \quad 80 \quad 92 \quad 101 \quad 232$$

Or, plot the data on a number line. Before drawing a number line, look at the range. Use the least and greatest values in the data set to determine how to set up the number line.

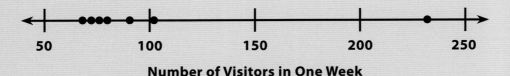

Number of Visitors in One Week

Notice that most of the data are clustered close together. One data point is far from the others. This is called an **outlier**. What was the median number of visitors to the gift shop for the week? Do you think the median describes this data set well? Why or why not?

Idea 3: Find the Mean.
The **mean** is an average for a set of data. It describes what the value of all data points would be if all the data were "evened out." Here is one way to find the mean:

Math Camp Week	No. of Students
Week 1	28
Week 2	25
Week 3	20
Week 4	24
Week 5	23
Week 6	27

First, look at the data showing students who attend Math Camp over six weeks.

Next, find the sum of the data points. This is the total number of people who attended Math Camp.

$$28 + 25 + 20 + 24 + 23 + 27 = 147$$

Each week is a data point in this set of data. There are six data points in this data set. To find the mean number of students per week, divide the sum, 147, by the number of data points, or 6. What was the mean number of students per week who attended Math Camp? Do you think the mean describes this data set well? Why or why not?

Idea 4: Find the Mode. Sometimes the **mode** is a useful number for describing a data set. The mode is the value that occurs most frequently in a set of data.

For example, look at the following line plot. It shows the ages of students working in a group at Math Camp.

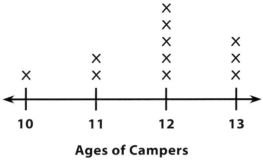

Ages of Campers

What is the mode of this data set?

Do you think the mode describes this data set well? Why or why not?

Idea 5: Use a Chart or Table. Sometimes data are in word form. For example, Math Camp students sometimes count animals that visit certain spots in the park. This helps the rangers manage wildlife in the park.

A **tally chart** is one way to note data that are in word form. Look at the following tally chart. It lists how many of each animal a Math Camp group counted at one wildlife observation station.

Animal	Number Seen
skunk	|
raccoon	|||
squirrel	ⱠⱠⱠ ⱠⱠⱠ ||
fox	|
deer	ⱠⱠⱠ
chipmunk	||

A mode can be determined for this set of data. It will be a type of animal, rather than a number value. What is the mode for this data set? Note that it is possible for a data set to have more than one mode.

Do you think the mode describes this data set well? Why or why not?

Materials

- **3 number cubes**
- **counters, various colors**
- **paper**
- **pencil**

An Average Game

Use the number cubes to create a set of numbers. Roll all three number cubes at once. Add the numbers that you rolled. Record this sum. Roll all three number cubes again. Record the sum again. Continue until you have 4 sums. These are the numbers you will use for this activity. You can also call them data.

Pick up a corresponding number of counters for each number. This will give you four stacks of counters. Now, rearrange the counters to make the stacks even. This may or may not be possible, depending upon the numbers you rolled. If there are counters left over, imagine dividing them equally among the stacks. This is a hands-on model of the mean.

What's the Word?

Like many English words, *data* comes from Latin. The root *dat–* means "a given thing," that is, an object or observation. The suffix *–a* shows more than one, or a plural. So, we say "data <u>are</u>" and "the data <u>show</u>." The singular form of *data* is *datum*.

Next, use an **algorithm** to find the mean of the data. An algorithm is a series of steps you follow to solve a problem. First, find the sum of all of the numbers. Then, divide the sum by four. The **quotient** may or may not be a whole number. This is a calculated mean.

Repeat the activity, rolling the number cubes to make four new numbers.

Use the numbers you roll to find each of these measures:

- the range
- the median
- the mode
- the mean

Write the numbers in order from least to greatest. Subtract the least value from the greatest value to find the range.

Circle the number in the middle of the ordered numbers. This is the median.

Look for two or more numbers that are the same. This is the mode. The set of numbers you rolled may or may not have a mode.

Finally, use an algorithm to find the mean number of the numbers you rolled.

The Visitor's Center

Campers call it the Cabin.

The first stop for many people at the park is the Visitor's Center. It's a small building near the entrance to the park. People can find information about the park and sign up for walking tours.

When summer starts, the park gets very busy. People pay a small fee to enter the park. There is plenty of room for people who come just for the day. If people want to spend the night in the park, though, they have to sign up. They pay another small fee for a campground site. Or they can sign up to get a permit to go backpacking. They can do all of this at the Visitor's Center.

Next to the Visitor's Center is an historic building. It's known simply as the "Cabin." The Cabin was someone's home more than a hundred years ago. Now it's part of the park. The Math Camp students meet here for classes.

Rangers keep track of the number of visitors. One Math Camp assignment is to use the rangers' data to find the average number, or mean, of visitors to the park.

The chart to the right shows the number of visitors to the park for the first eight weeks of summer last year.

These data show that the number of park visitors changed from week to week. That is to say, the number of visitors was different each week. In fact, it was different each day! There are several questions we can ask and answer about this set of data.

Week	Number of Visitors
1	1090
2	579
3	917
4	397
5	1078
6	921
7	903
8	695

Find the least value. Find the greatest value. What is the range for this data set?

For this time period, what was the average number of visitors to the park per week?

After finding the average, plot all of the values on a number line. Then, plot the average in a different color. Compare the average to the least and greatest number of park visitors per week during this period.

Another project math campers start with is creating a data set. One of the early projects is to list the colors of the shirts everyone is wearing on their first day of camp. The campers put their data in this tally table.

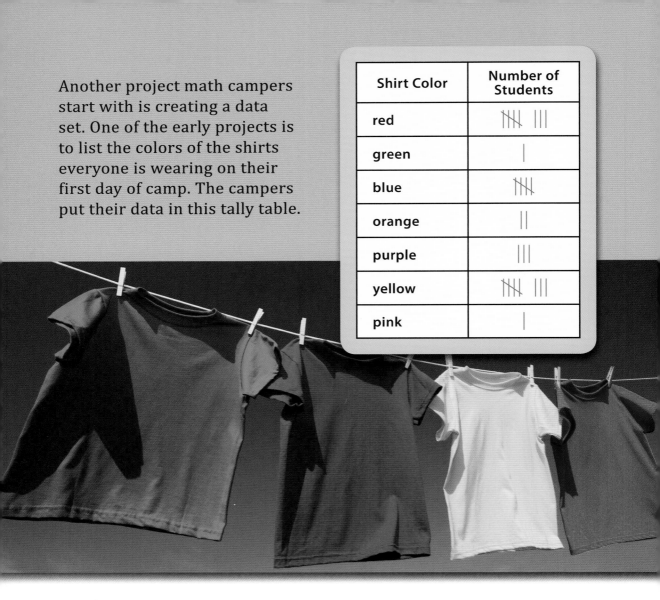

Shirt Color	Number of Students
red	卌 |||
green		
blue	卌
orange	||
purple	|||
yellow	卌 |||
pink		

For this data set, each tally mark stands for an observation. An observation measures one or more characteristics, such as the color of an item. What is the total number of observations that make up this set of data? What colors are the most common, or what is the mode for this data set?

Week 1: Find the Rubber Duck

Each group looks for a hidden rubber duck at the end of their week at Math Camp. To find the rubber duck, math campers have to first solve a problem. Once they solve the problem correctly, they get an envelope that holds a clue to finding the rubber duck. This is the problem for Week 1:

Ratios are sometimes used to create or describe data. A ratio is a comparison of two numbers or measures using division.

The ratio of camp leaders to campers is $\frac{1}{6}$, also written as 1:6. This means there is one leader for every six campers. If all of the campers cannot be organized into six groups of equal size, one more leader is needed for a new group. If the campers for Week 1 totaled 56 campers, how many leaders would they need?

The Week 1 campers get the answer right! They head out to find the rubber duck. They find it in a pond near the Visitor's Center.

Checking the Weather

People who manage parks pay close attention to the weather. Weather affects the number of visitors each day. When weather is pleasant, more people are likely to do things outside—like go to a park. When weather is cold and wet, more people are likely to stay at home.

Rangers at the park have a weather station. Math campers look at data from the weather station each day. A weather station is a group of instruments, usually set up on a box or stand of some kind. The one outside the Cabin includes a thermometer, a **weather vane**, and an **anemometer**.

The thermometer measures temperature. A weather vane rotates to show from which direction the wind is blowing. An anemometer measures wind speed.

An anemometer has three small cups on short rods. The cups catch the wind, which makes them spin. Weather stations are usually connected to a computer. The computer measures how fast the anemometer spins, which tells the speed of moving air.

Rangers depend on weather stations like this one to collect information about wind speed and direction.

Meteorologists are scientists who study weather and climate. They gather data from weather stations all over the world. They pay attention to the high and low temperatures for each day.

The computer for a weather station records the temperature at regular intervals. Math campers look at the temperature data. It is given in degrees Fahrenheit (°F). The students make graphs and describe the temperature data.

A camper made the following line graph. It shows temperatures for a June day (24 hours) at the park.

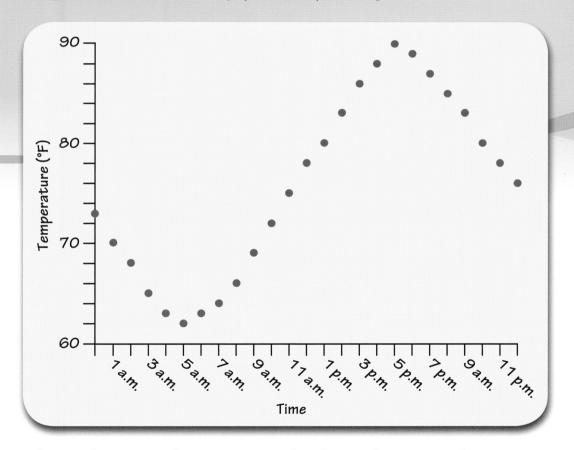

What is the range of temperatures for this 24-hour period?

Math campers take data from a previous year and describe it. Then, they show the data in a double line graph. This graph shows the average monthly high and low temperatures for one year at the park.

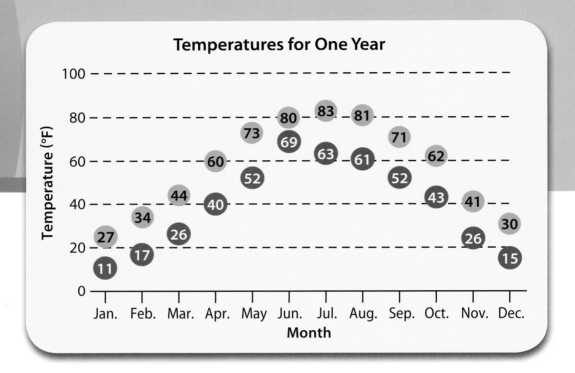

Before they graph this year's data, the campers must find a total of twenty-four data points. They need to find the average high temperature for each month. They also need to find the average low temperature for each month. What are the best methods for finding these answers?

Many people from a region report weather data. Computers send other data automatically from weather stations. Organizations such as the U.S. National Weather Service collect all the weather information. Scientists describe the data and keep track of long-term patterns for temperature, winds, and other weather data.

18

Week 2: Find the Rubber Duck

The campers in Week 1 hid the rubber duck for the Week 2 campers to find. Camp leaders created a data problem for them to solve. They took data that park rangers had collected for eight days, while measuring rainfall in the park.

The graph below shows rainfall amounts per day. Amounts were recorded to the nearest quarter inch. Are the data clustered or very spread out? Are there any outliers?

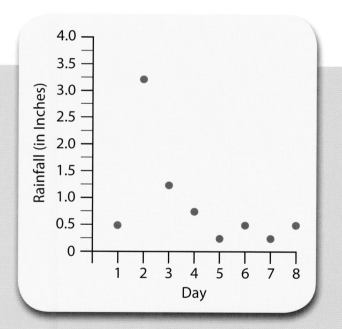

 **Did You Know?**

Natural rubber comes from tree sap, and is collected in the same way maple syrup is. In the late 1880s, people found a way to manufacture rubber. Thousands of uses for rubber have been found since, such as making toys. The earliest rubber ducks were hard rubber and did not squeak. Today, most "rubber ducks" are made of plastic.

The main question the campers had to answer for a rubber duck clue was: What was the median for this set of data? Note that there is an even number of data.

The Week 2 campers answered correctly, and were quickly off to find the rubber duck. They found it underneath the weather station.

Many people visit the park just for the day. Others stay overnight in the park. During busy times of the year, it's best to call the park ahead of time to reserve a place to stay.

The park has two campgrounds, where people can drive or bike in and set up a tent. There are also a few small cabins that people can rent.

The park is next to a state forest. Some of the forestland is wilderness. This means there are no buildings or roads, and trails are not maintained as well as trails inside the state park. But people can hike into the wilderness with their backpacks and camp in certain places.

Rangers keep track of how many people use the campground and cabins, and how many people go backpacking in the state forest "next door." They study the data from several years at a time. They can use the data to estimate how busy different parts of the park will be at different times of the year. And of course, students who come to Math Camp get to play with the data!

In the campgrounds, there are a total of 48 spaces for people to stay overnight. There are 42 camp spaces and 6 cabins.

Recall that a ratio is a comparison of two numbers, using division. What is the ratio of the number of cabins to the number of camp spaces?

During the summer, rangers give nature talks at the campgrounds several nights each week. Park employees also check the campgrounds several times each day. They empty trash cans and make sure the restrooms are clean. They make sure everyone has registered and paid camping fees, and they answer any questions campers may have.

The cabins are becoming more popular. Visitors have suggested the park add more. However, there is no more space for cabins. So, park managers are planning to replace some camp spaces with cabins. They plan to build enough cabins to make the ratio of cabins to camp spaces $\frac{1}{6}$. There will still be a total of 48 spaces in all. How many cabins will there be?

Backpacking is a great way to spend time out in nature. It takes more planning than camping in a campground. A person must carry everything she or he needs in a big backpack. Backpacking trails are often more challenging than trails used for day hikes. They are often steeper, longer, and more rugged.

A few spots in the park provide good access to backpacking trails in the neighboring state forest. Backpackers sign in at the visitor center. They tell the park rangers where they plan to hike and when they plan to come back. Rangers keep track of the number of backpackers. If people don't come back on time, rangers go looking for them to make sure they're safe. Also, knowing how many people are staying in the forest helps rangers know how much of the land is being used.

Here are data on the number of people who registered to backpack between June 8th and June 14th, last year and this year.

	Jun. 8	Jun. 9	Jun. 10	Jun. 11	Jun. 12	Jun. 13	Jun. 14
Last year	3	10	8	4	2	3	6
This year	2	9	5	8	6	2	8

What is the median number of backpackers for June 8–14 last year?
What is the median number of backpackers for June 8–14 this year?

Week 3: Find the Rubber Duck

Math campers must wear sturdy shoes for most activities. They can wear running shoes or light hiking boots, for example.

The Week 2 campers hid the duck for the Week 3 campers. Camp leaders also surveyed their group for data to give to the new campers. They asked Week 2 campers to report how many shoelace holes they had in one of the shoes they were wearing one morning. Then, they graphed the data.

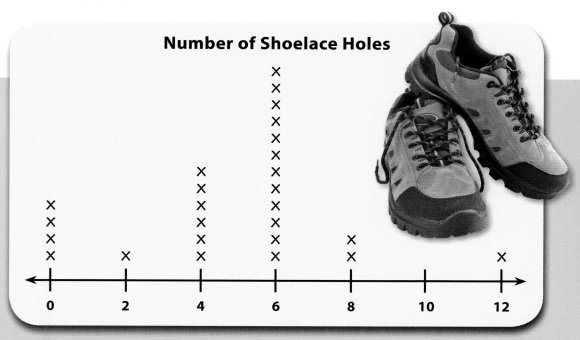

Number of Shoelace Holes

What was the mode for this data set?

The Week 3 campers got the answer right away. When they opened the envelope, they found a direction to search outside one of the little cabins at the campground. It took them a little while, but finally they found the rubber duck hidden in a stack of rocks next to the cabin door.

About 3,000 bison live in Yellowstone National Park in any one year.

CONNECTING TO HISTORY

A national park is an area of land set aside by a national government, for use by all people. Like state parks, national parks are places that are special in some way. Often they are especially beautiful land, are historically important sites, or are set aside to help preserve wildlife. Some parks are all three.

The first established national park in the U.S. was Yellowstone National Park, created in 1872. Volcanoes were once very active in the park. Great heat in the earth below Yellowstone affects groundwater. A geyser is a hot water spring that boils from time to time, sending a column of extremely hot water and steam high into the air. Yellowstone is famous for its geysers, wildlife, and natural scenery.

About three million people visit Yellowstone each year! Park rangers and employees manage the visitor centers, trails, and campgrounds. They also monitor wildlife. In 1916, the National Park Service (NPS) was formed. It now manages 58 national parks and sites around the United States.

Banff National Park was Canada's first national park. It was established in 1885.

Mexico's first national park was Parque National Desierto de los Leones, or Lion's Desert. It became a national park in 1917. The park is in the Sierra de las Cruces Mountains, right next to Mexico City. Altitude in the park ranges from 2,600 to 3,700 meters (8,530 and 12,140 feet) above sea level. The park has a relatively cold and damp climate, with forests, meadows, small river canyons, and waterfalls.

Banff National Park was the first national park in Canada. The Canadian government made Banff a national park in 1885. More than four million people visit Banff National Park each year to hike, camp, climb mountains, ski, and visit the hot springs. Banff is now part of a cluster of Canadian national parks. Together, these parks make a World Heritage site.

Exploring the Park

Most trails in the park are natural dirt, kept clear by the frequent passing of booted feet. There are also a few paved paths near the Visitor Center. Along the paths are a pond and different patches of plants. Visitors can take a guided walking tour along the paved trail with a ranger, who talks about plants and animals that live in the park.

For the walking tours, one ranger takes a group of up to twenty people at a time. The rangers think they should cut the number of guided walking tours. This will give them a little more time for other duties. So, they looked at data regarding times that people take the tours.

The guided tours are usually offered Wednesday through Sunday, at regular starting times. The rangers recorded the number of visitors on tours for four weeks. They then figured out the mean number of people on a tour at each time.

Assume rangers will stop giving tours for times when the fewest people attend. What time is the least popular?

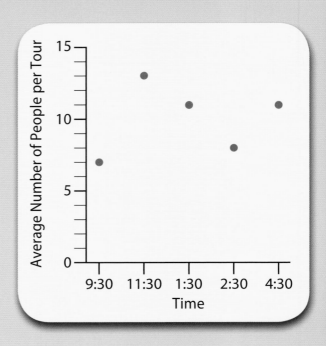

Rangers are responsible for knowing the conditions of all trails in the park. They often hike the trails themselves. Sometimes it's also useful to know how much a trail is being used. Math Camp leaders give students a chance to collect data at least once during their week at camp.

Math campers spend some time at the beginning of a trail, or trailhead. Trailheads and branches in trails are often marked with a sign. Students work in groups of 3 or 4, with a leader or ranger. They stay at the trailhead and count the number of hikers who enter and leave the trail there. The trails connect in different places, so hikers can go in one place and come out in another.

Here is an example of combined counts a group of math campers made at trailheads one day.

During the time math campers counted, which trailhead was used least? Which trailhead was used most?

Trail	Hikers In	Hikers Out
Mullein	7	2
Ridge	16	20
Bonnie	10	11
Starlit	2	8
Froux	8	2

Park rangers wanted to find average use for all trailheads. They set up metal tins, pencils, and pieces of paper at all trailheads. They put up signs asking visitors to help them research trail use. They asked visitors to write down which trailheads they used each day. People then turned their information in to the Visitor's Center before leaving the park.

Data were collected for two weeks at a time. The total number of visitors using the Ridge trailhead for this period is given here.

Day	1	2	3	4	5	6	7	8	9	10	11	12	13	14
Number	23	21	19	18	12	15	8	21	17	22	16	20	21	33

What is the average number, or mean, of people using the Ridge trailhead for this period?

Most of the values in the data set are similar to the average. Identify the outliers.

Week 4: Find the Rubber Duck

Camp leaders measured the heights of the campers in Week 3. For their rubber duck clue, campers in Week 4 worked with this data. They used the data to create the following histogram. A **histogram** is a bar graph that shows the frequency of data arranged in intervals. The histogram below shows the frequency of data, or campers, within intervals of five inches.

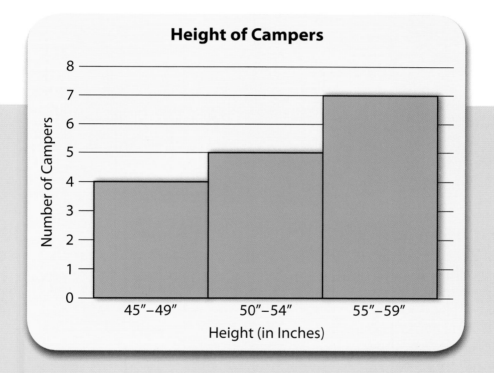

Then, leaders asked the campers to answer the question: How many students had their height measured for this data set?

The Week 4 campers discussed the question for a while. But they got the correct answer with no difficulty. Soon they were following their clue to the Mullein trailhead. There they found the rubber duck buried under a small pile of rocks.

At the Lake

Park visitors enjoy many activities at the park's largest lake. People come to simply sit on the beach, to swim, picnic, and use various kinds of boats. Students get to play at the lake too, as part of their week at Math Camp.

The most popular lakeside activity with the math campers is kayaking. Camp leaders make sure everyone has a life vest and paddle. The campers take turns learning how to move and turn the kayaks.

At the end of their kayak sessions, math campers are asked to look around the beach. They are asked to come up with questions that can be answered with data sets. Remember that the number values in a data set have **variability** and a range, and they can be described using some type of average.

Math campers write down their ideas for questions. Which of the following sample questions can be answered by creating and describing a data set?

a.	What is the temperature outside right now?
b.	What are the ages of all the people on the beach right now?
c.	Which activity are the most people taking part in?
d.	What day of the week is it?
e.	How does the number of people swimming compare to the number of people using kayaks?

There is an area of picnic tables near the lake. Visitors are asked to keep food and related trash away from the actual beach. But the picnic tables are available for everyone to use. People come from the beach, hiking trails, and Visitor's Center to have lunch at the lake picnic area.

Math campers are often given the task of describing picnic area use. They have to come up with a question and then answer it with data they collect. For example, they can ask, "How many people use the picnic tables each hour?" Students can then answer the question by collecting and describing data.

One week, math campers decided that they would count people at the picnic area on one Tuesday. They organized themselves into groups of three or four. Each group watched the picnic tables for an hour. This meant the campers still got to do other camp activities throughout that day of Math Camp.

The results of their data are shown in the table below.

Picnic Table Usage

Time Period	Number of People
10–11 a.m.	15
11 a.m. to 12 p.m.	11
12–1 p.m.	22
1–2 p.m.	16
2–3 p.m.	7
3–4 p.m.	14

What is the range in the number of people using the picnic tables during the one-hour periods? What is the average number, or mean, of people using the picnic area over the whole time that students counted?

Week 5: Find the Rubber Duck

For the Week 5 campers, camp leaders made up data. They did this by taking turns rolling number cubes. Each person rolled five number cubes at the same time, and then added the numbers on top of the cubes to get one data point.

The following table shows the sums that the camp leaders rolled for this made-up set of data.

Roll	1	2	3	4	5	6	7	8	9	10
Sum	17	13	21	17	16	19	19	15	17	17

What is the mean for this data set? What is the range? What is the median? What is the mode?

The campers had to answer all four questions correctly, which they did very quickly. In the envelope were directions to the picnic area by the lake. They found the rubber duck taped to the bottom of one of the picnic tables.

Watching Wildlife

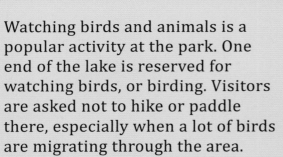

Bird	Number Seen
Duck	ⵍⵍⵍⵍ |
Canada Goose	ⵍⵍⵍⵍ ⵍⵍⵍⵍ ⵍⵍⵍⵍ ⵍⵍⵍⵍ ⵍⵍⵍⵍ ⵍⵍⵍⵍ ⵍⵍⵍⵍ |||
Gull	ⵍⵍⵍⵍ ⵍⵍⵍⵍ |
Heron	|
Loon	ⵍⵍⵍⵍ ⵍⵍⵍⵍ ⵍⵍⵍⵍ
Other	ⵍⵍⵍⵍ ||

Watching birds and animals is a popular activity at the park. One end of the lake is reserved for watching birds, or birding. Visitors are asked not to hike or paddle there, especially when a lot of birds are migrating through the area. However, bird-watchers can use small structures called "blinds" to observe the wildlife. A blind is like a wall, with small openings. Visitors can hide behind it and look through the opening with binoculars, or take pictures.

Of course, many animals may still sense that people are in the area. But when they cannot see movement, the creatures are more likely to hang around where people can watch them.

Birding is one activity that math campers can choose to do. The chart above shows the number of birds one group observed on a trip to the park's bird-watching blind. What was the mean number of bird sightings?

People also go birding in the forested areas of the park, away from the lake. Some birders can identify birds by their songs. Hiking in the park, they may hear bird song, and then stand still to see if they can spy the bird.

Birding is more popular in warmer months, since many birds migrate to warmer places or are less active during winter. There are simply more birds to be observed in spring and summer! Birders usually keep a list of birds they've seen in nature. If birders can identify a bird by its song, they count that as an observation. If they can, birders often photograph birds as well.

Below are data for the number of chickadees that birders reported along Starlit Trail over a ten-day period.

Day	1	2	3	4	5	6	7	8	9	10
Number	34	38	27	21	30	25	40	17	36	29

What is the mean for the number of chickadees counted per day? What is the median number of chickadees counted per day? What is the mode?

A chickadee

The park has another blind that visitors can hike to along a short trail. It is built among the trees, near a creek. It's a scenic spot that animals frequently visit, which makes it a great place to take nature photographs. So, the small structure is called a "photo blind."

Math campers can come to the photo blind to collect data. They commonly observe animals such as deer, various birds, squirrels, and chipmunks. Then, rangers give them a list of all animals that have been seen in the park. Students learn that some animals are most active around sunrise or sunset, such as rabbits and porcupines. Others, including foxes, bats, and raccoons, are usually active only at night.

Students at Math Camp and many visitors are only in the park during the day. If they collect data on animals in the park during the day, they are missing a lot of animal activity. This means their data are not a good sample of *all* animals in the park.

A blind in the woods

MATH AT WORK

Park rangers work all over the world. Park rangers use math daily.

Rangers often work directly with park visitors. They collect entrance and camping fees from visitors. They may have to calculate the rate at which people are taking maps and brochures. They have to know how many must be ordered and how much this will cost.

Park rangers often work with scientific data. They may record and report weather data, such as the amount of rain and snow at the park. Rangers also use weather information from meteorologists. If the weather will be extremely hot, rangers post warnings for people to drink plenty of water and keep cool. Or if severe storms occur, rangers may be responsible for closing trails or parts of the park.

Rangers participate in other scientific work. Scientists and park managers often count the number of certain animals or plants that live in an area. This helps to keep track of how well wildlife is doing. In large parks in Africa, for example, rangers sometimes need to move animals. They may need to give an animal medicine to fall asleep first. They have to calculate the right amount of medicine to give, based on the animal's approximate weight.

Keeping Active at Camp

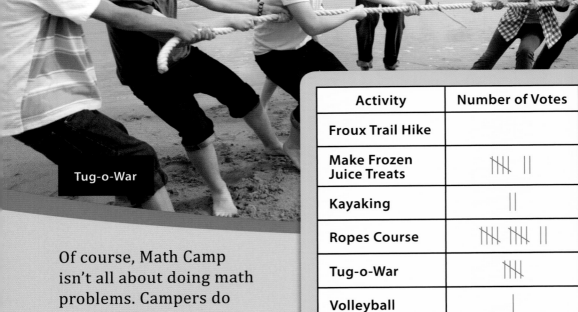

Tug-o-War

Activity	Number of Votes
Froux Trail Hike	
Make Frozen Juice Treats	||||| ||
Kayaking	||
Ropes Course	||||| ||||| ||
Tug-o-War	|||||
Volleyball		

Of course, Math Camp isn't all about doing math problems. Campers do many kinds of activities. On the last day of their week at camp, each group is given a list of activities they can choose from. Everyone gets to vote on which activity they most want to do. The whole group does the three activities that get the most votes.

Students in Week 6 of this summer's Math Camp voted for their activity choices, as shown in the chart. How many observations make up this set of data? Which activity did math campers choose the greatest number of? What activity had the second greatest number of votes? The third greatest?

The Week 6 campers played Tug-o-War first. They mixed up the teams with each round and dragged each other across the beach until they started to get tired. Then, they took a break and went indoors to the Cabin's kitchen. There, each student got to fill two plastic molds with his or her favorite juice flavor. It takes some time for juice to freeze, of course. So, they went out to play on the ropes course while their juice pops formed.

To do the ropes course, every person must wear a helmet. When moving through the course, people are sometimes a little way above the ground. For these sections, a person is always tied in to a safety line, but wearing a helmet is still important for safety. Also, the sections that are off the ground are a challenge for some students—many people don't like heights! So, the ropes course can be a mental as well as physical challenge. But it's always fun.

The ropes course has a beginning and an end. Each math camper gets to move through the whole course at her or his own pace. Campers keep time for each other, so everyone can try to beat his or her own time.

The course starts with walking across a rope strung low to the ground, with additional ropes to hold on to for balance. Then, campers have to go over and under a series of ropes. They walk or crawl across a rope net, then climb another net onto a tower. From there, they walk across a rope higher off the ground. After a few more challenges, they exit the course and rest.

The following histogram shows a group of math campers' ropes course times on their first turns.

In which time, in minutes, did the most campers complete the ropes course?

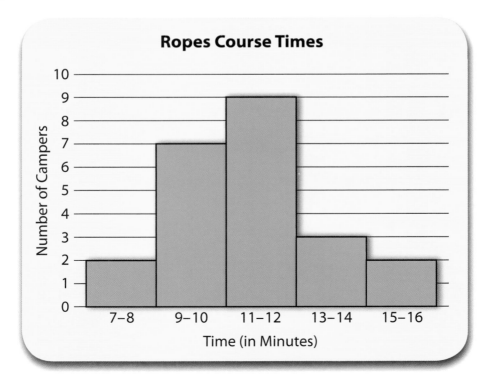

Week 6: Find the Rubber Duck

Week 6 was the last week of Math Camp for the summer. The Week 6 campers got to test themselves against previous groups. Camp leaders had recorded the length of time it took other groups to find the rubber duck.

Campers in Week 6 were given the following data:

Week	Time to Find Rubber Duck (in Hours)
1	0.75
2	1.25
3	2.0
4	1.75
5	1.5

What is the average time it took other groups of math campers to find the rubber duck?

The Week 6 campers worked together and answered their question quickly. Their clue took them to the photo blind. They found the rubber duck tucked into a corner of the blind, and in less than average time! They thought this was a perfect way to finish Math Camp.

At state parks and national parks with lakes, rangers and managers need to know how many people use canoes and kayaks on the lake each month. That's because, in some places, the number of boaters may have to be limited. For example, rangers may want to make sure that migrating birds that are in the park for a short time are not disturbed.

The rangers looked at boating data from a full year. They looked at Visitor's Center records and added up the number of people who said they were planning to canoe or kayak in the park. Rangers wrote this data set on sticky notes so they could arrange the data easily.

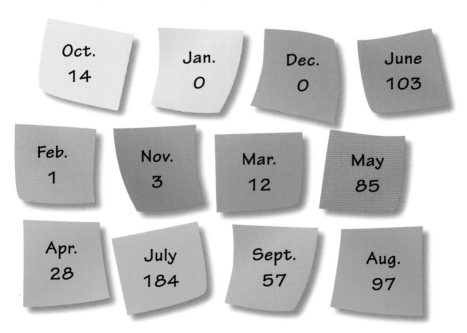

Think about a method the rangers could use to find the times when the most people canoe or kayak in the park's water. Will specific descriptions, such as range, median, mean, and mode, help them answer their question?

Idea 1: Find the Range. Math campers help the rangers interpret this data set. First, they organize the sticky notes to find the **range** of the data. The range of the data is the difference between the greatest value, 184, and the least value, 0. So, the range for this data set is 184. But this information doesn't tell rangers the months that the most people are canoeing or kayaking in the park.

Idea 2: Find the Median. Next, the campers find the **median**. To find the median, they arrange all of the values on the sticky notes from least to greatest value. A number line is also useful in some cases. But in this case, math campers find it simpler and quicker to rearrange the notes:

$$0 \quad 0 \quad 1 \quad 3 \quad 12 \quad 14 \quad 28 \quad 57 \quad 85 \quad 97 \quad 103 \quad 184$$

There are two middle values, so math campers add them and then divide by 2 to get their average:

$$14 + 28 = 42$$

$$42 \div 2 = 21$$

The median value describes the center of a set of data. But it's difficult to know what this description says about all of the data.

Idea 3: Find the Mean. Finding the **mean** tells the math campers what the average number of people using canoes and kayaks would be each month if they were spread out evenly over the whole year.

The sum of the data is 584. There are 12 data points, so, to find the mean, the math campers divide the sum by 12:

$$584 \div 12 = 48.7$$

This value is very different from the median. Also, for managing human activity on the lake, knowing the number of canoe and kayak users per month evened out over a year won't help rangers know when to restrict boating activity.

Idea 4: Find the Mode. A **mode** is a value that occurs most often in a data set. In this case, only 0 appears more than once, so 0 is a mode for this data set. However, 0 is not a useful number for this problem.

Idea 5: Use a Chart or Table. The median, mean, and mode don't describe the data in a useful way for the rangers. The easiest way to identify the most important description of the data is to use a chart, in which the numbers of people using canoes or kayaks are organized by month. The chart makes the answer obvious, so it is the best way to answer the rangers' question. In which two months do the most people canoe or kayak in the park?

Month	Jan.	Feb.	Mar.	Apr.	May	Jun.	Jul.	Aug.	Sep.	Oct.	Nov.	Dec.
Number	0	1	12	28	85	103	184	97	57	14	3	0

You don't have go to a Math Camp or be a ranger to find numbers outdoors. Watch birds from a window, picnic in a neighborhood park, or play games with friends. There are data all around you.

Foresters are people trained to manage forests and take care of trees. Foresters and other scientists may measure individual trees in a larger group of trees. Certain measurements tell them how healthy the trees are. If trees in an area are not healthy, foresters may remove them or do something else to help the trees in the area.

Foresters may measure the heights of trees. They use a small instrument that they can look through. The instrument tells them the angle at which they are looking at the top of a tree. They can then measure how far they are standing from the tree. A forester can use these measurements and a kind of math called **algebra** to calculate the height of a tree. Foresters may also measure the **circumference**, or distance around, a tree trunk. They make this measurement 1.4 (4.6 feet) meters above the ground.

Scientists share their data. Foresters, **botanists**, and other scientists who study trees are familiar with many studies and data. They know the average height and circumference of a healthy tree of a certain species.

Think about ways to measure the health of a group of trees. What kind of data need to be collected? What tools are needed for measuring and recording data? How will the data be described and shared?

GLOSSARY

algebra: a part of mathematics in which letters and symbols represent values in equations and algorithms, or formulas.

algorithm: a method, or series of steps, for solving a problem.

anemometer: an instrument that measures wind speed.

average: a single number that describes all the numbers in a data set.

backpacking: a form of camping, in which people carry everything they need in a large backpack.

botanists: scientists who study plants.

circumference: the distance around a circle or circular object like a tree.

data: information, usually in the form of numbers.

data point: one piece of information in a set of data.

foresters: people trained to manage forests and trees.

histogram: a bar graph that shows the frequency of data in intervals.

mean: the average value of a data set, found by dividing the sum of a group of addends by the number of addends; an average.

median: the value that falls exactly in the middle of the range of values in a data set; an average.

meteorologist: a scientist who studies weather and climate.

mode: the value that appears most frequently in a data set; an average.

outlier: a value in data set that is much lesser or greater than most of the other values in the set.

quotient: the result when one number is divided by another into groups.

range: the difference between the greatest and least values in a data set.

ranger: a person who works in a state or national park or a wilderness area; works to manage the park resources and keep visitors safe.

ratio: a comparison of two numbers (usually measurements) using division.

tally chart: a table that lists items and uses tally marks to represent each observation.

variability: how much the values in a data set are spread out, or vary.

weather vane: an instrument that shows wind direction; usually a rod with a wide flat piece on one end that rotates freely.

FURTHER READING

FICTION

Holes, by Louis Sacher, Dell Yearling, 2000

Tug-of-War (Summer Camp Secrets), by Katy Grant, Aladdin, 2010

NONFICTION

Collecting Data in Animal Investigations, by Diana Noonan, Capstone Press, 2010

Data, Graphing, and Statistics Smarts!, by Rebecca Wingard-Nelson, Enslow Publishers, 2011

ADDITIONAL NOTES

The page references below provide answers to questions asked throughout the book. Questions whose answers will vary are not addressed.

Page 7: 80; 24.5

Page 8: 12 years old

Page 9: squirrel

Page 13: The range is 693. The average is 822.5.

Page 14: 28; red and yellow (the data set has two modes)

Page 15: 10 leaders (56 divided by 6 is $9\frac{1}{3}$)

Page 17: 28 °F; The range is the difference between the high (90 °F) and low (62 °F) temperatures for the day.

Page 18: For each month, find the sum of high temperatures for all days of the month, and divide this by the number of days in that month. Repeat this process for the low temperatures.

Page 19: The data are mostly clustered. Yes, there is an outlier of 3.25 inches on Day 2. The median is 0.5.

Page 21: The ratio is $\frac{1}{7}$ or 1:7. There will be 8 cabins.

Page 22: Last year's median is 4 backpackers. This year's median is 6 backpackers.

Page 23: The mode is 6 shoelace holes.

Page 26: 9:30 a.m.

Page 27: Least—Mullein; most—Ridge

Page 28: The mean is 19 people. Students will likely identify two apparent outliers as 8 (Day 7) and 33 (Day 14).

Page 29: 16 campers

Page 31: Questions b., c., and e. can be answered statistically.

Page 32: The range is 15 people. 14.17

Page 33: The mean is 17.1. The range is 8. The median is 17. The mode is 17.

Page 34: The mean is 13 birds.

Page 35: The mean is 29.7 chickadees. The median is 29.5 chickadees. There is no mode.

Page 38: 27 observations total. The activity with the greatest number of votes is the Ropes Course; Second greatest: Make Frozen Juice Treats; Third greatest: Tug-o-War.

Page 40: 11–12 minutes

Page 41: 1.45 hours

Page 44: June and July

INDEX

CONTENT CONSULTANT

David T. Hughes

David is an experienced mathematics teacher, writer, presenter, and adviser. He serves as a consultant for the Partnership for Assessment of Readiness for College and Careers. David has also worked as the Senior Program Coordinator for the Charles A. Dana Center at The University of Texas at Austin and was an editor and contributor for the *Mathematics Standards in the Classroom* series.